MW00938934

Luxury Home Sales for the Digital Age

Harness The Power of the Internet to Sell Your Home In Record Time!

Ryan Harper & Sondra Harper

Luxury Home Sales for the Digital Age

Copyright © 2014 by Ryan Harper & Sondra Harper

All rights reserved. No part of this book may be reproduced or transmitted in any form or by any means without written permission from the author.

Table of Contents

Part I. Internet Marketing Basics

Part II.
Putting the Basics to Work, Online Lead Generation

Part I

Introductions &
Internet Marketing Basics

Chapter 1

The Who? What? Why? When? And How?

Who and what you are "in the real world," may seem an unusual way to measure success in the cold world of internet marketing.

But knowing who you are dealing with behind the machine is as important now as ever!
Internet marketing for real estate has some powerful tools, and we use some of the best, but even the most advanced power tool is worthless, in the hands of an unskilled carpenter.

That is the approach that my wife Sondra and I take to the complex word of Colorado Real Estate. It is a cutting edge, yet "holistic" approach that does not leave "holes".

I like to describe the local real estate market landscape in the Boulder Colorado area, as the Wild West! It's a land grab on the Internet. But, with the right people in your corner, you will get the results you want and deserve.

I'm Ryan Harper, and my wife, Sondra Harper and Coldwell Bankers welcome you and hope you'll find our hospitality here as good as gold, with answers to the very questions you have.

Growth is about years and the effort you put in, and Sondra and I have grown our online and offline business and numerous other businesses for now over 7 years. Our success is based on our unique approach that leverages the everywhere presence of the internet for new lead generation, while maintaining the human touch where it counts.

Yes, everyone's on the internet, but not everyone knows without wasting valuable time, just where to go, what to do and "blam", see those results coming in--like magic.

But, it's not magic, or rocket science, it is skill and experience that *we* put to work for *you*! It comes from our 100 plus hours of research and testing, and our own created unique marketing methodologies--that work.

I answered friends and strangers who asked me, "how do you do it?" with my first published book, *SEO and PPC Unleashed*. And now, this book is the home base of it all--how to dominate in the local real estate market and specifically the luxury home market.

Why the luxury home market in boulder Colorado? What is prominent about life in Boulder, Colorado is that the average home price is over 600K and climbing. Plus, it is a smart move to cover some costs that are involved in a marketing plan...and, luxury market sales does do that!

Why this book?

Simply put, our proven, results driven systems, are our passion. We have used these tools to change our lives for the better, and we want to do that for others. It is our way of giving back. Let's roll with this book and you will see, for sure!

About the Authors

What do you get when you combine the outside the box ingenuity of an entrepreneur with the focus of an engineer and the heart of the benevolent US Navy Veteran?

You get Ryan Harper.

Ryan Harper began his life's mission as an Eagle boy scout at early 14, and proudly served this nation for four years aboard the USS Enterprise. After his honorable discharge, he started an electrical contracting business that soon grew to millions of dollars in sales.

With business savvy, he leveraged the electrical contracting business to become a builder of high end custom homes. His new company built and sold 17 homes for over 8.5 million dollars in less than 18 months!

Never one to rest on his accomplishments, Ryan sold that business and pursued a career in Internet Marketing. Now he is recognized by Google as an expert in the field--in fact he "wrote the book!: His book co authored with Matt Lewis, "SEO and PPC Unleashed," is the "must read" for any business owner who wants to understand the ins and outs of online marketing.

Yes, there was pride in serving the needs of our country, but now, Ryan's overwhelming pride is right at home in his backyard so to speak, serving the Real Estate needs of the Boulder area. It is in fact his unparalleled internet skills that work the magic to find you the home of your dreams, or to quickly sell your home at the price you want!

There is no better reward for Ryan at the end of the day, then knowing he has helped to improve his client's lives by achieving their real estate goals.

Personally, he enjoys spending time with his family, wife Sondra, two children a cocker spaniel named Truffles, and fitting in some martial arts, hiking, fishing, four-wheeling, and scuba diving.

Sondra Harper uses her unparalleled intuitive senses and skills to have become a Red Ribbon professional master of the Feng Shui Guild. Feng Sui, the rare art of ensuring optimal positive "vibe" if you will, energy, ambience, comfort and life to a home, especially the interiors.

Her abilities serve the real estate needs of the boulder area by being able to evaluate the needs of clients and recognize the attributes of each property--from the depths of the inside out!

For Sondra, Feng Shui reveled itself to her as not just an art to appreciate, but necessary to each persons physical, emotional and spiritual life in their property. She found that out the first time she lived in a home that was uncomfortable to say the least. She used what she learned, and miraculously the environment changed, and the happy home owners were able to sell this property at a price they loved..and of course, they loved Sondra, as well!

Her studies at sacred sites the world over--learning about formations and land energies, her knowledge and appreciation of each property encompasses her wise, holistic understandings.

She is a featured consultant with Golden Gate School of Feng Shui.

Additionally, to add to her multi dimensions, for a well-balanced home and life of her own as well as her clients, she is a yoga instructor, and a master practitioner of Neuro-linguistic programming.

Sondra is happily married to Ryan, they are the parents of two children and a dog. Their life's work is balancing each other's unique strengths in providing besides their own family and friends, with sustainable solutions for a well-balanced home and life.

A quick warning:

I don't use Google, Facebook, Admob, Adroll or any other ad platforms the way that most other Internet Marketing Gurus preach about. These are my tested and true techniques that I have learned over the years and what I currently use in my business today.

So, if you have millions of dollars to spend on ads and don't care if they convert to leads or ultimately a sale. If you are looking to "Brand yourself" online.

This book is not for you!

However, if you're looking to get a campaign up and running quickly and start generating leads today and you don't mind that I am not an English major. ☺

Let's get started!

Notes

Chapter 2

Choosing the Right Platform

Every realtor new or experienced decides whether or not to go it alone or hang their hat with a larger brokerage. Having been self-employed for the last 14 years, I have a new found appreciation for being "subsidized!"

I used to think that everything needed to be in my control and if it was not my idea, it probably would not work. But at least I was open to learning and a change of mind. The truth is, in the real estate industry you can build your own company plus have the backing of a giant dedicated to helping you succeed. Now, whether or not you choose Coldwell Banker, Century 21, Keller Williams, ReMax etc. plays a big part in your success.

That decision was easy for me right after my interviews with several Brokerage firms.

Why Coldwell Banker?
Besides being number 1, training and Previews!

The Coldwell Banker Choice:
From Splendor to Fantastic Fantasy-- The Luxury of Rare Property

Here's what could be a script for a viral you tube video:

"It's for sale on that yellow brick road!" "Near us or another country? Let me guess, is it...
a) the Emerald City Castle,
b) the Chateaux de Chillon,
c) Playboy Mansion,
d) H. Keith Norton's Spy Mansion,
e) Carnegie Family's Smithsonian Design ,
f) Barbie's Dream house?"
or,
g) your property?"

Whether they're real or imagined, you can't dispute that this is a rare list of properties. But the list is a match for the "rare" abilities of Coldwell Banker and Coldwell Banker Previews International.

There is no luxury property--fantasy or real-- that is above or beyond the reach of Coldwell Banker and Coldwell Banker Previews International.

Since 1933, CB and CBPI have been leaders in matching buyers and sellers around the world of rare luxury properties such as stately castles, remote islands, mansions and exclusive estates.

CB and CBPI know how every property is built with a story and a dream. Like Disney, CB, and CBPI are good at telling your property's unique story. The numbers of their daily sales might even sound like the fantasy numbers of the height of Jack's beanstalk home or the depth of Ariel's coral Castle!

Naturally, CB and CBPI aren't about kids' fantasy and fairytales--they are just not stodgy and stuck in rigidity, or, those who don't innovate, and who let obsolescence set in. You want movement in the right direction. CBPI is creative and personable, moving forward with the latest marketing tools and bonuses to match your personal wishes, with your best buyers.

It is exactly how CB and CBPI became a go-to number one, for luxury and ultra luxury international properties-- one of the worlds most comprehensive and sophisticated luxury home marketers.

The Art of It All: CBPI chosen as selective connoisseurs who highlight the beauty of your property
"Describe the property", they ask. "Well, it's inside and outside, has space and closure, the

geometrics have rectangles squares, ovals and parallelograms...and the material is...".okay, stop stop" Why? Because...this is *not* a description from CBPI. CBPI knows how to describe the *life* of a property. Every property does breathe its particulars--for the connoisseur of it all! And the beauty connoisseurs of CBPI began long ago.

It all began with the movie script sounding, but real history, of Coldwell Bankers Previews International. The colorful biopic of CBPI began with entrepreneur Henderson Talbot, a lover of motion pictures during the depression of 1933. His genius saw that previewing gorgeous real estate in gorgeous pictures was a unique and exclusive means to highlight the nuances and distinctiveness of the properties. And we all know about the picture's worth! He turned his camera on properties of exceptional design and character, to "preview" these homes to national and international buyers. Moving forward, the name and the ingenious use of innovations and marketing have continued and grown with CBPI.

Bankers Previews International brings the sophisticated cultured glamour of the movie spotlight to your home--the star. They are the red carpet of Luxury Property Real Estate, for the sale of exquisite and unique property customized by their proposal to you, a proposal of their qualified strategies that will market your home to the most qualified buyers--worldwide.

Henderson Talbot's ingenuity moved real estate marketing mountains even more. He was the first marketing innovator to go beyond local listings and highlight his distinctive properties in national and international publications.

Your Exclusive Marketing Menu

- CB will arrange to have one of its preferred photographers capture minimum 25 HDR magazine grade images with motion tours
- Your property is seen in Two proprietary magazines. Homes and Estates Magazine has a 90,000 print distribution to affluent in the US, including ultra-high net worth individuals, newsstands, international airline lounges, private jet facilities, email to those with $19 million+ net worth.
- Unique Homes, the magazine of luxury real estate, is on newsstands and bookstores worldwide, reaching more than 300,000 readers in the US and in 80 countries, and also in the digital publication.

- Multiple property photos are viewed through: CaliforniaMoves.com,ColdwellBanker.com. ColdwellBankerPreviews.com NYTimes,com.OpenHouse.com,Realtor.com, Trulia.com,Yahoo!RealEstate,Zillow.com,Fron tDoor.com,HomeFinder.com,WSJ.com,Homes .com,AOL.com,UniqueHomes.com,PrimeLoca tion.com,FindaProperty.com,and RobbReportCollection.com

- CBPI is the first national real estate brand to launch its own you tube channel, cold well banker on location, with now more than 8.9 million video views worldwide.

- Your own feature 60 second TV spot and you tube video is produced and viewers will see it and fall in love by millions on TV Sunday mornings at 9:00 following the nationally syndicated show, Today's Homeowner on Colorado's Channel 2. Your You Tube video will be streamed online 24/7 on the top real estate sites worldwide.

- Super-Sized Announcement will be produced and mailed, 5.5x11 "Just Listed card to 50 addresses around your home. The love for a beautiful image personally received in the mail has never died.

- The brochure bruha. Of course you will have a creative designed magnificent 4-page UV coated property brochure, featuring your home--a must-see property.
- Quarter page advertisement in Colorado Homes and Lifestyles Magazine mailed to 32,500 paid subscribers and read by 97,500, plus additional 19,380 online viewers.
- The connections--of CBPI worldwide is unparalleled--...a network of 3,100 offices in 49 countries and territories, covering more international locations than any other brokerage firm.
- CB has more than 10,000 certified specialists working worldwide.

Counting up Kudos

The numbers talk the talk and walk the walk. Here are some figures for you--no need to memorize, just so you know how CBPI is working for you in "countless" ways.

- CB Independent sales associated handled more than 20,000 transaction sides of homes priced at $1 million or more in 2013, averaging $102.7 million in luxury home sales every day, totaling more than $37.5

billion in sales annually and $288 million in luxury sales locally.

- CBResidential Brokerage in Colorado participated in more than 180 transaction sides of homes priced at $1 million or more in 2013 totaling more than $288 million in sales.
- In 2013 CBPI listed nearly 10,000 homes valued at more than $2 million, with 25% of those listed for more than $4 million.
- CBPI sold two of the top five most expensive properties in the US in 2013: Casa Casuarinas in Miami-the former home of the ate Gianni Versace--and The Crescent Palace in Beverly Hills.
- In 2010 CB was the only brand to sell on of the top 10 most expensive homes in the US "Le Belvedere" originally listed for $85 million Previews has a track record of being selected to represent 3 out of 5 of the priciest homes in the US
- CB sold more than 3,385 million dollars plus luxury properties in Northern California, accounting for more than 6.4 billion in sales of luxury homes sold there.
- CB worldwide referral network has over 460 international offices in 51 countries, territories and possessions

The Pulse of new tech and traditional values beats strong for CBPI.

Everything old is new again as CBPI combines the old-world know-how of 70 years of innovation with the latest in high-tech marketing tools.

- CB is spending $3 million on search engine advertising which includes 95,000 search terms on the major sites. More than 92% of home shoppers use the internet as part of their home search.
- CB powerful web exposure syndicates your home to 700+ websites worldwide.

CBPI partners target 52,000 prospects with direct mail campaigns. These include owners of aircraft, yachts, horses, fortune 1000 executives, investors and decision making executives of over 10-25 million individual net worth.

Making Connections – Around the Corner, and Around the Globe.

- Yes, with the Previews micro site, CBLuxury.com in China, Russia and the Middle East.

- Superb global agent network, referral system over 460 international offices in 51 countries, territories and possessions
- CB today sells more million dollar properties than any other real estate company in the world. Marketing includes personalization afar with several relocation and referral services through a network and a principal broker for Cartus Relocation, the #1 relocation company worldwide After all, the world is small and 27% of traffic to CBP.com more than 8,000 luxury property listings is from visitors outside the US.

Rare Homes Deserve Rare Qualities CBRB sales associates uphold their reputation for expert guidance, individualized service, attention to detail, and know that you deserve these qualities, the highest level of professionalism and discretion to protect your privacy and interests.

Their marketing plans are built and customized, just like each property is built and customized to the uniqueness of buyers and sellers. For a one of a kind client and one of a kind home.

State of the art tools and technology--CBPI rocks the media!

- The social media is still growing, and CB has an extensive online and social media network covering all the major sites. And, the CB Mobile Brochure sends texts to any prospective buyer's mobile device in seconds.
- You will have your own property website. Because CB recognizes your home, they create your exclusive single property website with your own personal URL.
- Enhanced technology is the thing, including Showcase Enhance, makes for increased traffic and ease in your listing and marketing.
- With CBPI you get a program that is powerful enough to reach distant shores, and sophisticated enough to find luxury homebuyers where they live and work with

Representing rare and unique Colorado Real Estate takes "Real" expertise, the kind you will find with CB and CBPI!

Chapter 3

Understanding the different parts of Google

Before we go any further, let's take a look at a search engine results page. For this example, we will use Google since they have the majority of the search market (well over half at the time of this writing).

Sponsored Listings: The sponsored listings are companies or individuals that are participating in Google's Pay Per Click program or PPC. They are called sponsored listings because they have sponsored the right to be listed when a specific keyword phrase is searched. To get your business listed here you need to implement a PPC program and setup an advertising budget.

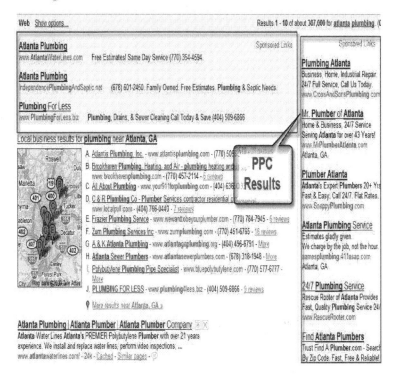

Local Results: The listings here are typically for service related business and show people searches based on their geographical location. Google can determine your location based on where your Internet connection is located. This is great for local business! They now can get showcased right where the searchers are looking for them.

Google atlanta plumbing   [Search] Advanced Search
                                       Preferences

Web Show options...   Results 1 - 10 of about 307,000 for atlanta plumbing. ((

Atlanta Plumbing   Sponsored Links   Sponsored Links
www.AtlantaWaterLines.com   Free Estimates! Same Day Service (770) 354-4594.
                                                                                    Plumbing Atlanta
Atlanta Plumbing   Business, Home, Industrial Repair.
IndependencePlumbingAndSeptic.net   (678) 601-2460. Family Owned. Free Estimates. Plumbing & | 24/7 Full Service. Call Us Today.
                                                                                    www.CrossAndSonsPlumbing.com
Plumbing For Less
www.PlumbingForLess.biz   Plumbing, Drains, & Sewer Cleaning Call Today & Save (404) 509-6866   **Mr. Plumber** of Atlanta
                                                                                    Home & Business, 24/7 Service
                                                                                    Serving Atlanta for over 43 Years!
                                                                                    www.MrPlumberAtlanta.com
                                                                                    Atlanta, GA

Local business results for **plumbing** near **Atlanta, GA**

A. Atlantis Plumbing, Inc. - www.atlantisplumbing.com - (770) 505-8570 - 28 reviews
B. Brookhaven Plumbing, Heating, and Air - **plumbing** heating and air ... -
   www.brookhavenplumbing.com - (770) 457-2114 - 5 reviews
C. All About Plumbing - www.your911forplumbing.com - (404) 636-5033 - 33 reviews
D. C & R Plumbing Co - **Plumber** Services contractor residential commercial -
   www.localpull.com - (404) 766-0440 - 7 reviews
E. Frazier Plumbing Service - www.wewanttobeyourplumber.com - (770) 784-7945 - 6 reviews
F. Zum Plumbing Services inc - www.zumplumbing.com - (770) 451-5765 - 16 reviews
G. A & K Atlanta Plumbing - www.atlantagaplumbing.org - (404) 496-6791 - More
H. Atlanta Sewer Plumbers - www.atlantasewerplumbers.com - (678) 318-1948 - More
I. Polybutylene Plumbing Pipe Specialist - www.bluepolybutylene.com - (770) 577-6777 -
   More
J. PLUMBING FOR LESS - www.plumbing4less.biz - (404) 509-6866 - 9 reviews

📍 More results near Atlanta, GA »

Plumber Atlanta
Atlanta's Expert **Plumbers** 20+ Yrs
Fast & Easy, Call 24/7. Flat Rates.
www.SnappyPlumbing.com

Atlanta Plumbing Service
Estimates gladly given.
We charge by the job, not the hour.
samesplumbing.411easp.com
Atlanta, GA

24/7 **Plumbing** Service
Rescue Rooter of **Atlanta** Provides
Fast, Quality **Plumbing** Service 24/
www.RescueRooter.com

Find **Atlanta Plumbers**
Trust Find A Plumber.com - Search
By Zip Code. Fast, Free & Reliable!

Atlanta Plumbing | Atlanta Plumber | Atlanta Plumber Company
Atlanta Water Lines Atlanta's PREMIER Polybutylene **Plumber** with over 21 years
experience. We install and replace water lines, perform video inspections, ...
www.atlantawaterlines.com/ - 24k - Cached - Similar pages -

Organic Listings: This section is where the sites that Google deems worthy according to their proprietary algorithm live. To get a website listed here SEO is used. The basics and general concepts are here in this book and are enough to get you started on the path to achieving an organic listing on page one of Google.

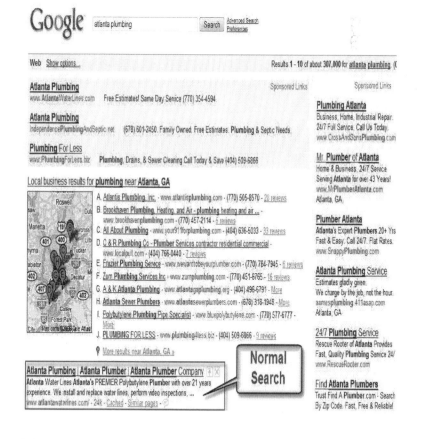

Maybe you've been using Pay-per-click (PPC) advertising and making some money doing so. This method has proven to be successful. However, while you can make good money using PPC, you'll be able to make great money with SEO. With SEO we're getting your information placed where most people browsing on the Internet are going to look. Heat map studies that track eye movement on a web page have shown that the majority of time is spent on the upper left hand corner and then down the left side of a search engines results page. PPC ads do get attention, but you're missing out on most of the hottest "spots" in the heat map – which are shared with the top position (most costly) PPC advertisements and the subsequent organic (SEO) results. You need to get your information into the location on the pages where it's going to get the most attention. This means much more to you as a business owner. Utilizing PPC is a great method to purchase traffic for your website but adding SEO to your marketing mix will further impact and increase your revenues.

Google Heat Map:

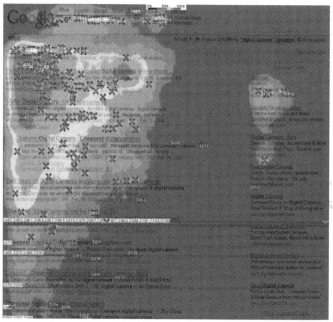

Notice the highest paid sponsored position and the top three SEO results get the most attention; this is where you want to be!

The biggest question in Internet marketing is "How is your next customer going to find you?" If your customers can't find you, you'll soon have no business for them to find. If you've been using the yellow pages to attract customers, your methods are out of date. People are searching for the things they want using online searches. In fact, a recent survey showed that 41% of all people who were searching online were looking for local businesses.

After all, shipping charges can be expensive, and a lot of people would prefer to buy locally and avoid the extra costs – if they are able to find what they're looking for locally. People look for services at a local level because they do not need a plumber in Canada when they live in Southern California. In fact, recent changes to how Google shows their search results automatically takes into account your geographical location, ultimately making your local centric website more effective than ever before.

Recently comScore published that <u>over 40% of all searches</u> on the Internet were "close to home". Out of these searches over 1/2 of them were focused on a specific business!

"Two out of five local searchers (41 percent) were looking for information on a <u>local service in their home area</u>, including car rental office, dry cleaner or lawyer."

If that information doesn't make you think twice about how you may position yourself to capture some of these customers **"LOOKING"** for <u>your service</u> then this certainly will!

This is what comScore found: "**performing a local search drives consumers to take action.** During the second quarter of 2006, 47 percent of local searchers visited a local merchant as a result of their search behavior, while 41 percent made contact offline. More than one -third (27 percent) made contact online as a result of conducting a local area search."

It only makes sense that you need to get your information out there where the browsing public is looking. Lots of people drink their morning coffee while perusing the Internet. How many people do you know that drink their coffee, pull out the 10 pound yellow page book and start browsing? You want to get the name of your business listed in the Google local search results and the normal search results at the top of page one. You want to use the right keywords so that when people do a search for services that you offer, they can be led directly to you.

Notes

Chapter 4

Getting Your Business listed

The best place to find the most attention right now is on Google. You need to face the fact that Google is where it's all happening. For example, if you are a plumber and want to let everyone know where to find you, you need to get on the local search results on Google so that a search for a plumber in your area will lead the customer right to you. The key is in knowing how to get your name included on the list. You can't just request that Google put you on there, because they have their own algorithm based on such things as keyword searches and reviews. The first step is making sure you are actually listed in the local listings with Google and if you are not, then the first thing you should is set one up. If your listing is already there, and you didn't put it there yourself, then it has been pulled in by Google from other business directory sources and may or may not have accurate information. If this is the case, then the first thing you should do is claim your listing, so you can edit it whenever you like, add coupons, pictures, videos, special offers and target the proper keywords.

www.google.com/business/

While you are at it, go ahead and submit your business listing to both Yahoo and BING. This will further leverage the local search capability and get you more customers!

https://smallbusiness.yahoo.com/local-listings

Notes

Chapter 5

How to build a link

Submitting articles to various article directors, blogs and other websites can get you a lot of attention. However, you need to constantly feed these sites new material to keep people interested. Fresh content is important, but it can definitely be hard to organize and keep up. You are probably wondering where you get all of this new content. Many businesses never achieve a high position ranking on Google at all, because Google has never heard of them. You don't want to let that happen to you. Although no one really understands exactly how Google goes about deciding who will be listed first, second, and so on... I can give you the tips and best practices that you need to get noticed by Google this will ensure you for those top spots.

Using keywords as hyperlinks is an important technique that you can use to help bring your material to the attention of Google and to thousands of potential customers. For instance, when doing an online press release, you need to use the right keywords in order to draw customers to your website. You want your online content to have links to your website embedded in your content. By doing this, you are giving people (visitors) as well as the search engines a way to find your site. Every one of these links is like a vote for your website. The more votes you have out on the web, the more popular your website is! It is also important to make sure you select the correct keywords to insert into your links. By selecting the proper keywords you are basically giving the search engines a guide about what your site is if your site sells a specific item or offers a specific service, you would want to include the name of the item or the service as the keyword you enter into your link!

<a href="URL">KW</a>

This is the basic structure of a link and it is really quite simple. The "URL" section is the page that you want to point to or send a vote to. An example of a link is Http://www.MyBoulderHome.com and if a link was built with this URL in it, when clicked it would send the visitor from wherever they were on the internet to the My Boulder Home website! The KW is the actual phrase or keyword that shows up as the link – the part you click on. Since My Boulder Home specializes in local real estate marketing or selling homes in Boulder CO, it would make sense to select one of the following keywords.

1. Boulder homes for sale

2. Boulder real estate

3. Boulder real estate companies

4. Boulder real estate market

Let's go ahead and build a link so we can see exactly what it looks like!

<a href="http://www.myboulderhome.com">Boulder real estate</a>

See how easy that was! You can further target your keywords by adding your physical location. For example, if you only service a specific state or city, then you could add that in your keyword. This not only helps push you up in the search engines for that keyword phrase, but gives the visitor a very specific idea of what you offer and what your site is all about.

Chapter 6

On Site SEO

Most businesses don't have the resources to employ a team to implement the following practices. Outlined in this book is everything you need to get started with achieving high position rankings and the success that accompanies it will follow. In fact, once your site has had the SEO action applied to it, you will dominate your market.

All other businesses should look at outsourcing their SEO needs in order to get the very best results. When you outsource your SEO to professionals, you put yourself up there with the big companies that can afford internal search engine optimizers. You can have the same services and financial success for a much smaller cash outlay. Undoubtedly you've always known this is the type of shot in the arm your business needs, but did not know how to do your own SEO. You've heard terms like "keyword research", "competition analysis", and "on page optimization", but you don't really understand them much less have a clue to how to make them work for you.

Page structure and layout are critical facets of the SEO process, but most likely these things aren't in your area of expertise. Let's face it. No one knows how to do everything. Just the fact that you're in business shows that you have your own area of expertise. However, both time and experience factors come into play when you're marketing. You must know the strategies for proper keyword selection, or your SEO campaign may break down even before it gets started.

You have to create content with the right keywords and the proper density of those keywords. You need to know how to write and place image alt tags so that they will receive the attention they need, and you need to be able to set up a site map that will be both user-friendly and effective in steering customers to the sections of your website they want to find. If all of this sounds like a foreign language to you, you aren't alone. Probably 99.9% of all people have no clue to what any of this is or how to use it. Big companies are successful and make a lot of money because they can afford SEO pros, and I am going to share this information with you right now.

There is also another breed of marketer that is using the Internet to highly leverage their success and they are much smaller that fortune 500 companies. These fast moving individuals are small to medium sized business owners that have educated themselves and applied the principles found in this book – and have enjoyed the success that comes with it.

Here is a list of on page factors you must ensure are currently present, and if not, implement them immediately!

Title Tag: This may very well be the most important on page element in your arsenal for telling the search engines and the public what your page is all about! The information you put in the title tag is displayed at the top of the web browser when that page is viewed. Not only that, it is what the search engines display in their results page when people search for you! What exactly does that mean? It means that you had better put some serious thought into what you put here! It may be the first thing your customer sees about you and your business.

It is important for the title tag to serve two different roles, and balancing the two may seem like a daunting task. The keywords you want the search engines to see must be present, yet it must also be presented in a way that makes people want to click on it! Since people will see this boldly listed in the search results, make sure you put something compelling along with your keyword. If this wasn't challenging enough you only have a short amount of space to "get the job done". This is subject to change, but the general standard for title tags is 65 characters, keep it under this and you will be fine. Note that you can go above that character limit, but the search engines will only show the first 65 characters and will then ellipse the rest of the line. As a general rule, try your best to stay under 65 characters.

To make your title tag really zing, put a benefit in it!

Meta Tags: Back in the "dark ages" of SEO the Meta tags carried a lot of weight. This just isn't the case anymore. However, they still provide a benefit and value to your website and to your site visitor. In the search engine results, the Meta description is used to describe what your site is about. If you do not set one up, then the search engines will have to pull some text from your page and list it. While this might sound okay, what if the search engines pick up your shipping policy or a snippet of text that doesn't really do your product or offering justice? What if it does not tell the searcher how great your company is? Well, if you do not set this up for yourself, you really leave it up to chance. It does take a few minutes per page to set up properly, but making sure your future visitors have the right idea about your site is well worth the effort.

Put your phone number in your Meta description! There is a good chance the person searching for your service or product will just pick up the phone and call you – after all, if they are searching for it, they want it… Often right NOW!

One thing to mention about the Meta keyword entry is in the past webmasters would "stuff" all kinds of keywords in here, literally hundreds; it is now better to put a handful of keywords that specifically identifies the topic of that page.

In fact, my personal recommendation is, if the keyword you enter here is not actually in the content of your page – remove it! I also very rarely go over 4 to 6 keywords in here.

Title Tag

Dallas Plumbing Company
Dallas Plumbing Company offers Air Conditioning, Heating and **Plumbing** installation and service to North Texas. Our Kitchens and Baths **plumbing** fixture ...
Contact Information - Air Conditioning Service - Our Products
www.**dallasplumbing**.com/ - Cached - Similar - ☺ ⚑ ⊠

Meta Description

Dallas Plumbers in Dallas TX Yellow Pages by SuperPages
Directory of **Dallas Plumbers** in TX yellow pages. Find **Plumbers** in **Dallas** maps with reviews, websites, phone numbers, addresses, and business profiles.
www.superpages.com/yellowpages/C-**Plumbers**/S.../T-**Dallas**/ - Cached - Similar - ☺ ⚑ ⊠

Plumber Dallas Plumber Mesquite Slab Leak Locators Baker Brothers ...
Plumber - Baker Brothers **Plumbing** provides clean and professional licensed **plumbers** for leak location, drain cleaning, **plumbing** repairs and all pipe fitting ...
bakerbrothers**plumbing**.com/ - Cached - Similar - ☺ ⚑ ⊠

Heading Tag: Heading tags are the equivalent to the large bold print in a newspaper or magazine, it tells you the most important information about a piece of content and immediately lets you know what you can expect once you decide to read it. A heading tag also notifies the search engines what the content is about, in fact there are six different levels of heading tags. From heading one which is represented like this <h1> all the way down to heading six <h6>. The different levels signify the level of importance for that information. The <h1> is the most important of them all and also carries more weight than the other heading tags. The

49

information you put in here is critical to your onsite SEO success.

Sitemap: A sitemap is basically a list of all the pages on a website that the site owner wants the search engines to easily find. Sitemaps can be helpful in the planning stage of website creation but for our purposes we are going to be using them to enhance our rankings with the search engines. Google introduced sitemaps so that webmasters could publish a list of pages across their website. It really serves two purposes, it takes the load of the search engines to find every page on your site and it makes it super easy for the webmaster to say "here are the pages that I have created, in one place where you [the search engines] can easily find them". Bing, Yahoo, Ask and Google all use the sitemap protocol, so this makes it the most efficient means to update them when new pages are added to a website.

Recently a close friend asked me to take a look at his website, he is in the self improvement and personal development market and has built a rock solid business that does over 5 million dollars a year in sales with a staff of under six people – there is some really good ROI there! It bugged him that he wasn't on page one of Google for his most important keyword! He was there for a bunch of his secondary market keywords, but the main root keyword for his market wasn't there. This was mind boggling to him.

We sat down and took a close look at his site. I fully expected to find a couple of minute nitpicky things, but what I found was shocking! His heading tags were all messed up, even a junior webmaster or SEO consultant could have spotted this immediately!

He had phrases like privacy policy, shipping policy, order now, home business, all in h1 heading tags – remember, these are the MOST important ones!

The search engines didn't know what his site was about. They had a vague idea, but when they looked at the heading tags they were being thrown off big time. Effectively, it was like telling Google and the other search engines they were in the privacy policy, shipping policy, order now and home business? I just shook my head and wondered how this could have happened!

Needless to say, when I pointed this out to him, he was extremely shocked and up set! In fact, he was a little infuriated.. After about two minutes of anxiety, he calmed down, called up his webmaster and relayed everything I had told him so they could get it fixed immediately!

I am certain that once he gets his on page SEO factors reigned in and properly optimized he will start to see an increase in his rankings, and his already successful business will add more revenues and greatly experience more success.

Keywords: It is important to comment on the keywords for a moment. From the last story you saw the importance that telling the search engines what your site is about can make a huge difference in how it performs in the rankings. Picking the correct keyword is a critical step in getting you the results that you want. So much so, that we have dedicated a whole section to keywords along with the Pay Per Click (PPC) section. We walk you through step by step how to pick the best keywords and how to make sure they turn site visitors into buyers! Just keep that in your thoughts as your progress through all the information you are assimilating.

Chapter 7

Off-site SEO

Getting your information submitted to the right directories is going to make all the difference in the world when it comes to SEO. You need to know which paid and free directories can be the most critical to your expanding business, including local directories and yellow pages. You have to learn to understand ways to build 1-way, 2-way, and 3-way links between your site and others, how to submit articles, use keywords as hyperlinks, and how to utilize social media for your own purposes.

Don't beat yourself up about not understanding any of what you just read. Even the most successful businessmen and women in the world wouldn't understand it either. All of these concepts are relatively new, and it's not like we grew up hearing about them unlike today's generation of children. I didn't learn everything I know overnight, either. I learned SEO from the ground up and I'd like to see you succeed the same way that I have, because I have every reason to have you and your business thrive and flourish.

We're all anxious when we start a new business, and we want to see immediate results from our marketing efforts. After all, we're in business to make money, and making money means attracting customers. When I say that it takes a little time to get SEO working for you, how much time am I talking about?

Don't let any of this talk discourage you from considering SEO for your marketing needs, because there are a lot of proven methods we can use to get your business indexed and start your traffic moving. Some of these marketing methods include press releases, article marketing, link building, directory listings, and video marketing all, have shown over time that they can make a real difference in your business. Naturally, I don't expect you to know what all of these things are, because that's my job. I can not only explain these terms to you, but I can also show you how well they will work.

Let's go over these methods in greater detail:

1. **Press releases**: An announcement of an event, performance, or other newsworthy item that is issued to the press. The most important thing about press releases is you need to make sure you have something that is "newsworthy"! If you have done something significant in your business, then tell the world about it – press releases will often rank well in the search engines. You can add links in the press release that point back to your

site or page that is directly related to the topic of conversation in your press release. Another great reason to submit press releases is that in the process of getting more links to your site, local news agencies can often pick up your release and contact you directly for an interview. This is a great way to get the word out about your business, a new product, or service.

2. **Article marketing:** Article marketing consist of writing short pieces of content (500 to 800 words minimum) about a topic that is relevant to your business. It is important to make sure the quality of these pieces is top notch, they are like virtual salesman that work for you 24/7/365. The goal here is to provide value, not to sell. In fact some websites that host articles will not accept your article at all if it is just a sales pitch! You can still accomplish your desired goal; just ensure the content is informative and helpful. At the end of your article you have the opportunity to add a "resource box" which is a small snippet of text with a call to action as well as a link back to your website. A great call to action is to inform the reader that more information about the topic of the article is available over here. Then provide a link that

they can click on which directs them straight to your website. Let your website do the selling and close the deal. A key factor for success with article marketing is to make sure the article educates, informs, and enlightens about the product or service you offer and then when they come to the website to learn more – you can close the deal and give them an offer to purchase!

3. **Link building**: Link building is a broad topic, in fact every one of the items listed here in the offsite promotion section all deal with link building. That is how important it is! Here is the deal, the search engines really do not know too much about your website, they might have found it, checked it out, made up their minds what it is all about and then just moved on to bigger and more important websites. I know it sounds horrible and rather impersonal doesn't it! This is exactly why getting links back to your site is so important. The more links that you have coming to your site, the more important the search engines think your site is! It is similar in many ways to a voting system, when more people vote for a person running for office or a certain position that individual wins. The same goes for websites, the more "votes" or

in this case links to your site the better.
There are some technicalities in there as
well, it isn't quite as steadfast and simple as
that, but generally speaking the more links
you get to your site the better it will perform
and rank in the search engines.

4. **Directory listings:** Directory listings are an
   easy way to start building links to your site.
   These are sites that do nothing but list and
   organize sites into categories. The premise
   is that people will use these sites to find you.
   The reality is a small fraction of these sites
   actually refer visitors back to you. There are
   a set of directory sites that are high quality
   and very capable of sending you visitors but
   it is a small sliver of the directory sites on the
   Internet. This is a super simple way to start
   getting links back to your site. They are one
   way links, which means they do not ask for a
   link in return. These are the best kind! It
   takes a few minutes to enter in your
   information on the directory site but when
   you are done you will have a link. Get a
   bunch of these and it will go a long way in
   making sure your site gets noticed by the
   search engines.

5. **Video marketing:** Video marketing is one of the most powerful methods of getting traffic and attention to your website. It is also not as widely used and taken advantage of as some of the other methods listed here. One of the great things about using video is that the search engines seem to really like this kind of content. Often they will include "content listings" in with their search listings. Content listings include video! So often times, even for competitive keyword phrases a video will show up on page one of the search engines, where getting your site in the same spot would take a lot of work.

   Take a minute and think about it, would you rather read something, or just kick back, relax and watch a video? Most people would prefer to watch a short, informative video than read something. Not only is it easier but it appeals to more of the consumer's senses than plain text on paper or on the computer screen. Sight and sound can be combined to really enhance the delivery of content and make it much more compelling to act upon.

6. **Blog Posts:** Blogs have taken over the Internet! Chances are many of the sites that you frequent are actually blogs in disguise. I

say in disguise because it is really difficult to discern between a blog and any other website on the internet. Blogs are simply publishing platforms that allow content creators or site owners to deliver content quickly and easily. In fact they are so easy that you can log into the blog where a text editor resides and type up your blog post, make formatting changes to the fonts, add pictures or even embed a video. It is very easy to use and the very nature of blogs makes sure the search engines wake up and pay attention to your site. When a blog post is created it "pings" several sites basically alerting them that new content has been added. These different sites and search engines then run over to your site to see what is going on! Since blogs are easy to update and content is added regularly, the search engines have become enamored with them. Use this to your favor, if you don't have a blog setup to compliment your existing site then get one! If you are in the beginning stages of establishing your web presence, consider using a blog as a publishing platform for your content.

Another great thing about blogs is that you can use other people's blogs to create posts, or comment on existing posts and then insert a link back to your website. This is a great way to build credibility for your website. The most important thing to remember here is that in order for this to be effective you have to add value. So just don't post something off topic for the sake of creating a post and a link. The goal is to get the link, but in the process, read what they wrote, add a tip or trick that adds upon what was written or provide a resource that helps with the original subject. When you do this, not only will the comment you created be kept on the blog, the link will also. If what was written was helpful to someone, this person may click the link and go to your own website so they can learn more!

Links from blogs are a great way to increase your link count and help notify the search engines that your site has value!

All of the time you spend capitalizing on these successful methods will be time well spent when it comes to the future of your business. Look at it as an investment in your company. We've all heard that Rome wasn't built in a day, and that's true of any successful business, too. What we'll be building with SEO is a solid foundation that is going to prove invaluable to you as time goes on. I can help you find the best search terms that will really get traffic flocking to your business, and I can teach you to build landing pages for your keywords. All of these methods will bring results, and I know how to get them for you.

It's important to be at the top of the rankings on any search engine, and I've developed the techniques to get you there.

What I'm going to do is teach you how to set up your own blog. If you don't have a website, I'll give you guidelines for building one. If you do have one, I'll look it over for the glaring issues that are bound to be there but which are easy to fix when caught.

I can't emphasize enough that no one knows the methods Google uses to establish their rankings, because this information hasn't been divulged to the public. By doing extensive testing on our 100 plus website testing server I have established methods that I can guarantee will work for you. SEO can take weeks, months, and even years (for national and competitive markets) to show the results we're working for here, but when the results start pouring in, you're going to know that your patience was put to good use. Obtaining a high position ranking for a local based business is much easier than competing on the search engines for a nationally based keyword; you will see success often in 90 days or less for your local centric searches. You are investing in establishing the high Google rankings that will ensure your business will be flourishing for many years to come.

Notes

Chapter 8

What are the differences between SEO and PPC?

Okay, so why do some people utilize just PPC and others prefer SEO? I'm telling you that you need to use both. because when you put both of them to use in your business you then create the largest possible amount of leverage, attract the most possible customers and ultimately make more money than you ever could by just using one of them. Most cars today come with a four cylinder engine, which is great for most people. Just using PPC is also what a large portion of business owners do to attract customers to their website. If you could add another four cylinders to your engine and enjoy all the power and performance that came along with it, wouldn't you want to experience that? That is exactly what you are doing by adding SEO into your marketing mix. You are essentially doubling and often tripling the revenues that your site will generate for your business. Not only that, but both of those cars will definitely get you where you want to go, the question is… which one will get you there faster? Implementing both traffic generation methods will bring you larger amounts of success and significantly collapse the timeframes need to reach goals and business objectives.

Let's start by comparing the two methods and seeing how they stand up against each other.

PPC (Pay Per Click)

Pros:
- Instant Traffic

- Only pay for performance

- No fear of search engine updates

- Can easily test with multiple visitors

- Search engines treat you as a partner

Cons:
- Always pay for traffic

- Traffic limited to monthly budget

- If not constantly monitored can lead to negative ROI

- Click fraud can be a concern

SEO (Search Engine Optimization)
Pros:
- Free Traffic! You don't pay per click

- High volumes of traffic

- Highest ROI

- No bidding wars

Cons:

- Ranking can fluctuate

- Require time

- Cannot use a flash based website

- First page results for competitive keywords can be difficult to achieve

Our Suggestion? DO THEM BOTH!
Utilize both PPC and SEO in your business

As you can see, there are good and bad points when it comes to doing either PPC or SEO. This is why I believe in using both methods. By combining the two, you get the best of both worlds, and the negatives of one seem to be counteracted by the positives of the other.

For example, a new website can enjoy nearly instant traffic by utilizing PPC that can in turn also aid in identifying the best keywords for that particular market. Once this has been established, implementing these keywords for your market into an SEO campaign can provide consistent, long term search engine rankings and an abundance of visitors to your website.

Chapter 9

The Importance of Keyword Research

Having the right keywords is crucial to the success of any Internet marketing campaign. Most people don't have a clue about how to make the most of the use of keywords.

You first need to understand what your customers are looking for. What problems or needs drive their online searches? What types of inner conversations are they having with themselves? When you know these things, you can discover the keywords that are going to bring them to you. I can guarantee you that without having the right keywords, you aren't going to become as successful as you want to be.

There are two steps I will teach you to guarantee that you successfully uncover the best possible keywords to help attract customers for your business:

Brainstorm core keywords- this one is simple, just make a list of the words that you think your customers would type in Google to find you. (Your ideal keywords are the ones that people are using in Google, Yahoo, and Bing and are the keywords that get the most search volume, i.e. the most searches)

Take these main keywords from the brainstorm session and put them into the Google keyword tool, to find other related search phrases you never would have thought, and find out which ones get searched for the most.

Utilize free keyword planner by Google

https://adwords.google.com/ko/KeywordPlanner

Once we've determined the keywords with the highest traffic and Online Commercial Intent (OCI) then we can put these into our PPC (Pay Per Click) campaign, and after a short period of time we will know the words that "work". This means we will know the exact keyword phrases people use in the search engines for your services and even more importantly – the words they use to buy your product or services! This means that we will be putting all of the data that we talked about earlier into effect.

Let's get started:

Examine the domain name: It is often beneficial to have the main keyword for your market inside your domain name. There are two reasons for this; the first one is that it is one of the factors that help determine your search engine ranking from an SEO perspective. The second one is that this will immediately let your customers (site visitors) know what you are offering.

For example, www.dynamicroofing.com is much better than www.dynamicinc.com .

Can you see the difference? One tells you exactly what the company does, the other gives absolutely no indication about what line of work, service offered for product sold. The search engines view it the same way! There are other things you can do to clue in both the search engines and the site visitors and inform them what the site is about, but the domain name is almost always on all marketing materials and by having a clear message up front – there is less room for confusion about your message.

Remember we talked about writing articles and distributing them across the Internet? This is where the importance of keywords really comes into play. You want the message across your website and the content distributed over the web to have the same message or theme. That means keeping the keywords in mind when preparing your articles for distribution you create content for your website.

The same holds true for the blog on your company website. If you do not have a blog on your website, or do not know how to post on your blog – this is a great time to learn. Search engines seem to love blogs and the updated content they often bring to the web. This fresh content should also contain your keywords in it, so the search engines and your visitors know exactly what your site is all about.

Follow this approach in all the promotional methods that you employ! If you decide to participate in forums that are specific to your market, and where customers visit, make sure the language you use has your keywords in it. The search engines and the visitors reading your posts need to know precisely what you are referring to. When doing video marketing, or posting comments on another person's blog., the same goes for answering questions on Yahoo. You'll be doing this for 90 days and then repeating the entire process. You'll learn how to never let your marketing efforts go stale and will be providing fresh, new content for posting every single week. The search engines index content are actually content engines. They just love content! The more web content you provide on a consistent basis the better results you will have.

We need to make sure that your website is structured properly, I can't emphasize this enough! The page layout not only helps with SEO but PPC as well. Google is getting where it wants to reward marketers that know both SEO and PPC making it natural and relevant the way Google and other search engines want a site to be. You will learn to understand exactly what these search engines require in order to giving you top rankings.

Utilize the onsite elements from the on page SEO chapter to fully take advantage of integrating your keywords into your website. This is overlooked by 98% of your competition and this alone can give you the edge over their websites.

I know this is an awful lot to assimilate, but you won't be expected to learn everything there is to know in one sitting. As you learn the basic steps and build on them, you'll soon become your own marketing expert.

Chapter 10

PPC Adwords

As mentioned above, you don't want to discount using PPC advertising altogether, because you can benefit from using them in combination with SEO. You'll want to set up your first campaign on Google since they get the lion's share of the searches. This will allow you to quickly and effectively test your keyword selection and the ad creative that you develop. The faster you get through this phase the quicker you will start getting traffic to your site, and ultimately customers and dollars in your bank account. If you want to partner with Google and other search engines to provide your website with advertising, you have to remember they are very picky about what they want to see from you. The search engines have grading criteria called a quality score, which consists of numerous factors. Google publishes best practices for your adwords campaign but does not go into specific details regarding what this quality score is.. The gems of knowledge you are about to learn are what I do every day when I setup a new campaign and ensures that I will pass all the quality scoring with flying colors. If for some reason you do not pass the quality score test from the search engines, they will penalize you by making you pay more per click. Naturally, you want to avoid paying a premium price for your advertising, therefore you will need to learn the best practices of writing your ads.

There are some tips I can show you that will end up netting you lots of traffic with very little cost. Each advertisement you place on Adwords will consist of an ad title, ad text, and a display URL.

Why do we start with Google first for our Pay Per Click advertising?

Google can be your best friend when it comes to generating business. After all, it's estimated that the Google network reaches approximately 80% of all Internet users. If you've always thought of Google as being just a search engine, it's time to stop and readjust your thinking, because Google is just so much more. Millions of people use Google as their search engine of choice, and when they do, they also see your ad. The Google Network consists of Google sites & partner properties that use Google AdSense to serve content advertisements. These properties include: Search sites, content pages, newsletters, email services & discussion boards.

With the Google network, you'll be able to:
- Reach a large, highly-targeted audience

- Target ads to search results and relevant web content

- Opt in or opt out of search and content distribution

Now for the really big stuff. Here's what Google can do for you:

- Generate awareness

- Build brand

- Generate prospects / leads

- Customer acquisition

- Sales (make money)

As you can see, the purpose of the entire process is to generate the kind of sales that are going to increase your bottom line. When you advertise with Google utilizing their AdWords program, you reach millions of customers worldwide in over 100 different languages., or you can target a local audience all the way down to a zip code or a one mile radius around your physical location.

You'll always be able to reach the <u>right</u> audience with the <u>right</u> message at the <u>right</u> time.
Talk about power!

Search is the most dominant form of advertising on the Internet. Approximately 40% of all online advertising are search ads which shows that business owners are well aware of where their advertising dollars can best be spent. This form of advertising sees 73% penetration into the search network and users do an average of 35 searches per month. The number of people you can reach this way is truly staggering. Compared to other methods of advertising (i.e. banner ads, email, yellow pages, direct mail), search advertising is both affordable and effective.

The cost of search advertising is based on Cost-Per-Click (CPC). The way this works is that your ad is placed at the top or along the right side of the search page. You only pay when a potential customer clicks on your ad. Now you can probably see why using keywords and meeting the expected Google criteria are so important. If you're like most people searching the Internet, you've clicked on some of these ads. If the ad has been placed correctly and is on the right search page, the customer will probably spend some time looking at what you have to offer, because it's what they are looking for. However, if your ad isn't on the right search page, customers will click on your ad, find out it isn't what they're looking for, and go elsewhere. You still end up paying for their click even though they spent no time on your website. Placement of relevant ads means everything.

This last point is pure gold! All too often there is no congruence throughout the sales process and this is extremely detrimental to the advertiser (business owner)! The more you can line up the process and apply a common theme through your advertising funnel the better it will perform. For example, when the web surfer clicks on your ad and lands on your page, they find exactly what they are looking for . You will get rewarded with a new lead or a sale. This congruency is one of the things that search engines are looking for. Right out of the gate, you will enhance your campaigns with higher quality than your competition. Ultimately if your account gets a manual review by a quality assurance representative with the search engines, you will pass with flying colors and get their stamp of approval. This "blessing" will ensure that your marketing system will continue to work all day and night, 24 hours a day, regardless of what you are doing! That is an amazing tool for growing your business.

Another term that's important to online marketers is the CTR (click through rate). CTR is the method Google uses to measure relevance of an ad. By comparing the number of clicks versus the number of times your ad appears on Google or one of it's partner sites (impressions – how many times that page is viewed). Google takes this information and uses it to arrive at a percentage of relevance. Your relevance rating can then be compared to those of other search ads. You'll be able to know if your ads are working or if you need to tweak the information in order to increase your relevance. The more relevant your ad is when compared to your competitors' ads, the better placement your ad will get. The harder you work "with" the search engines to maintain your campaign quality, the more they will reward you.

The best way to get started with this is to sign up for a Google adwords account and get familiar with it. Make sure you walk through a campaign set up and get the complete basics (Google makes this part very simple). After you do that, I want you to read the following tips and implement them. They will drastically reduce your cost per click and ultimately increase your ROI.

1. Adjust your keyword bids in 1 – 3 cent increments. Increase the bids on an individual keyword basis until the keyword you are adjusting is at the position you want. Do this for each keyword individually.

2. Write your ad copy correctly:

    a. Put the keyword in the headline whenever possible

    b. Put the biggest benefit of your product or service in your ad copy

    c. Have a strong call to action – make it compelling

    d. Capitalize the first letter of each word in your headline

    e. Capitalize the first letter of each word in the display URL

    f. Local businesses list your phone number in the ad, they might just call and not even click

3. Make each keyword it's own add group (this separates your keywords and provides better tracking and metrics – search engines like this too)

4. Use all three keywords match types Broad ,Exact and Phrase for each keyword

5. Prune your keywords - don't keep keywords that are not getting clicks and get rid of non converting keywords (if a keyword isn't making you money or getting traffic, get rid of it)

6. Bid high at first to get the top position and then lower your price to what the average cost per click price is every few days. Keep your click through rate high and this will eventually lower your cost per click

7. After you have an idea of the maximum that you will probably pay and your campaign is converting where your want it, raise your daily budget to $1000 (This may sound frightening, but it will ensure that you get all the available traffic for the keywords you converted and put money into your business. This just opens the gate wide open and does not mean you will hit this budget daily)

8. Expand into the content network, set up separate campaigns and make sure you have no more than 50 keywords in each group

9. In the content network, make sure you go in to site and categories exclusion tool under topics and check the topics / conversations that you DO NOT want your advertisements

to show up in (Edgy Content, Conflict and Tragedy are some of the topics to exclude)

10. If relevant, use Geo targeting and add time scheduling to your campaigns

11. Create separate landing pages for each keyword or keyword groups. Example: If you are a dentist and you have an ad for Free exam and X-ray, don't send them to your main page. Send them to a page that tells all about your special offer along with sign up form and your phone number.

12. On a regular basis complete these steps, find new keywords to test and if some of your old keywords stop converting into sales, trim them from your marketing funnel.

(Wash – Rinse – Repeat on a regular basis)

13. Use Conversion optimizer (a tool inside Google) once you get 50 conversions or more per month. This turns your campaign over to Google where they will manage it for you and continue to lower your cost per click automatically.

Part 2

Putting The Basics To Work, Online Lead Generation

Notes

CHAPTER 11

How to Buy Leads For 5 Cents a Click

This is one of my favorite ways to generate leads and set us apart from the competition. The world is being taken over by the mobile device or smart phones. This is hard to argue against so why doesn't everybody have a mobile app ?

You're going to say, "I do, I can use the one my company has after I get a client." But what if you can use the app the same way you use your lead generating website?

There are a ton of companies out there that specialize in lead generating websites. Boomtown, Marketleader, Agentjet, Tigerleads,... Just to name a few. I personally use Agentjet and Marketleader. Since Marketleader comes with our Agent Value Package at Coldwell Banker, I decided to build my app with that. All of these companies will sell you leads but if you want to stand out and grow your business you will need to supplement with your own lead generation-- in my opinion.

Ok now for the big secret-- how you can create your very own app for free in 5 minutes or less. Are you ready ? It is a website called www.appsgeyser.com . This website is really a hidden gem. You can build an app out of any web page that is mobile friendly. This basically means that anyone can build an app. If you can copy and paste a url from your browser to the appsgeyser website, you can build an app.

What I did was take the mobile version of the Marketleader website that they built for me. This way everyone that downloads the app and starts searching for homes can sign up for new home alerts that will work on their phone, laptop, tablet, or desktop computer. This works seamlessly and gives the user a great experience.

To find the mobile version on a marketleader website just go to the bottom of the home page and there is a link that says "View Mobile Site." Go ahead and click that and it will give you the mobile version and the mobile url. Which should be www.yourdomain.com/p/ or at least that is what mine is now.

Now once you have that-- we need to go to appsgyeser.com and click on the big green button that says "Create Now" on the home page. After that it takes you to the create app page. You want to choose the "Website" option. Once you do that it will ask you for the Website url. Make sure you put in the mobile version. There is even a preview function so you can see how your new app will look. Hit the big yellow next button and you will need to come up with a app name. This should be easy ie "Colorado Home Search " or something that will stand out so people will know what it is when they see it.

Next step is the "description." This is where you need to type in the areas you serve like "Search for homes in the Boulder, Louisville, Superior, Longmont, Erie, Lafayette and surrounding areas." You get the idea-- you have 150 characters so make it great.

Next step is to get an Icon, they have default ones but who wants to use those. I know you probably are not a graphic artist but don't worry neither am I and I won't leave you hanging.

Go to one of my favorite places Fiverr.com and type in app Icon in the search box and for 5 bucks someone will create an Icon for you. Make sure to let them know that the size you need is 512 x 512 and check out the reviews. I normally wont use anyone that doesn't have at least 30-50 good reviews and I see something I like in their portfolio. This might take a few minutes but defiantly worth finding someone good. Now that you have uploaded your Icon click the "Create app" button and wall-la, you have an app. Just create an account on the next step with name, email etc.

Next step is to download it then publish it on Google Play store and Amazon Market place. Don't worry, this is all very simple. Appsgeyser has great checklists for the entire process. So I am going to just give you the highlights so we can get to the promotion part and generating real leads for 5 cents per click.

1.   Review your app compliance with Google Policy. There are 8 check boxes that you have to click on.
2.   Create screen shots of your app-- 4 or more. I used a program called snagit which let me take screen shots of the different search pages on the mobile site. I think it was $35 but there is a free one that I use sometimes called Jing by TechSmith www.techsmith.com/jing.html.
3.   You can translate your description to other languages.

4.   Download the "APK" file

5.   Create a Google developer account go to Google and type in "Google play developer account." Simple process sign up and pay $25. could take up to 48 hours. But hey how long have you been with out a app what is another few days. (I would do this part while you are waiting for your app Icon to be made.

6.   Publish it.

Ok now your have an app on the app store. Great! Now how do you get traffic to it? The answer-- Admob. There are others but Google bought Admob a few years ago and it is connected to your Google Adwords account. Sign up for Admob and click the promote new app button. Now don't get side tracked with the Monetize functions That is not what the purpose for this app is. You can go back later and make other apps if you want to make 2-5 cents per click. But for this app we want to pay for the clicks.

When you hit "Promote new app" you want to select an app. Type in the name of your app and it should appear as a selection. Select your app then you can select image ads or text ads. The simplest and fastest way is to do text ads but it you want fancy images-- again Fiverr will be the best place and when you select the "Image option," there is a "See supported specs" link. Click on that then copy the specs to give to your fiverr designer of the size you want. I like the text adds so come up with an ad name, max CPC or cost per click. I use 5 Cents. Now you need to come up with a catchy head line like maybe the name of your app-- Colorado Home

Search. You have 25 characters for this. Then on line 1 you have 35 characters and line 2 you have 35 more characters to describe why people should click on the ad. I think the best is to make it match your description. That way when they click on the ad they get what they are expecting.

Next you want to select targeting. "Geo Location", click on this for sure. You do not want all countries and territories. Select "let me choose." This can be tricky but you can narrow it down by City, State or the entire country. What I came up with that works the best for me is State. So if someone is in Colorado on their phone, my ad will show. I tried US, and the world, but it blew my budget up and I didn't see the conversions I wanted to see.

Next is "Languages" and since I only speak 3 languages, English, English Louder, English Slower, I selected English. If I spoke other languages I would add those.

"Carriers"-- I selected all carriers and WI-FI. Devices you need to change this to Android, so select "Let me choose Android" should come up, select "add all." You don't want to have your ad show up on IPhone, have them click only to find out they can't have your app. It will make them feel left out and possibly hurt their feelings.

"Demographics" is next All gender is fine but I do change the age to 25.

"Budget scheduling" and "name the campaign" is next. For the Daily Budget this is up to you-- $2 -$10 per day should do the trick. I have several campaigns and tested it for my market and $2 per day gets about 200 clicks per week and 5 downloads.

Notes

Chapter 12

Paying the Extortion Network

Once upon a time all a good relator needed to ensure that homeowners got the best protection and service for their property was savvy, a nice smile and good handshake!

But today, who can get along without technology that miraculously includes hundreds, thousands, millions, of other helpers to serve you and your clients. It's all right there at your disposal and in your face (no aspersions at all to face book) to ensure your clients get the best service and protection for their property needs and wishes. And when your clients get what they wish, you do too!

The smiles and the handshakes are still there, but now you need to use these tools to broadcast their homes to as many potential buyers as possible, to close their deals, answer their wishes, and ensure your job well done, and your needs and wishes also fulfilled-- a win win.

As realtors, aside from your intelligence and effectiveness with clients, you have to be intelligent about your best marketing shot and adding value. It is important to understand what makes the selling, the buying, and your business satisfaction and success as easy as possible. Then you will be recognized for your expertise.

When there are thousands of websites for buyers to find your home over a latte, how do you cut through the clutter and ensure the cream rises to the top? Who will drive traffic to your listings, how will your listing gain traction in search results?

The Buyers and Sellers Gist of Things

I know that today's syndication environment can be a spinning mass of confusion. It makes good sense to not spend time fighting against our syndication whirlwind--its our environment. Maybe, we should be welcoming it.

I like to think about what prospective sellers and buyers are doing and thinking. What's happening is our clients now have access to more information than ever before. Today, by the time clients contact an agent they probably have already spent time online researching neighborhoods and properties. Generation X and Gen Y clients are used to finding their info at their fingertips at an instant. There was a popular ad for a clothing chain many years ago that said, "An educated consumer is our best customer." We need to embrace that same idea!

From all reports, consumers love the big Z network-- Zillow, for their research. Zillow doesn't hard sell, no forced registration to view, no chat popups, no contact us for details button. Even when President Obama planned a forum on the housing market he met with Zillow CEO Spencer Rascoff. Zillow has the branding. Plug in a real estate term or search and you get Zillow near the top of the first results page.

If a seller client comes to you with a value that they saw online, they are doing their good thing, their research.

How to select your best shot at marketing value

Are you in or out of syndication networks? From its earliest beginnings in the 1800's, the original small group circle of the real estate information pool grew, and continues to grow in its ubiquitous network of information for buying and selling properties. This success obviously, is that the wider the reach of information and data exposure turns out to be about the best path to marketing success. If a property is found on hundreds of sites with national coverage, and your listing is promoted everywhere possible-- natch, your chance of selling homes more quickly to additional buyers pays off royally.

All much better than time spent worrying and attempting ways to drive traffic to your listings and to find other ways for your listings to gain in the search results.

It's accepting a kind of "if you can't beat 'em, join 'em mentality. By syndicating your listings you get the most widespread online exposure possible. No matter how stylish easy to use and full of info your website is, the average real estate brokerage website doesn't get over 5.5 million visitors in a month.

Brokers are great debaters.

Brokers are afraid of being replaced with the click of a button, like how blockbuster and book stores got taken out by the internet. But I think people will always want an expert when they are looking to buy a home. Nowadays, you have to be the expert online as well as with your winning personal ways, if you want to stand out and succeed. That smile and warm handshake just needs to extend through the screen!

The best choice will always be what is best for the customer-- how can we get their home sold in the fastest time for the most amount of money, which also has the graces of saving them the mortgage payments which, just go mostly to interest. This means getting their home out to the most amount of people in the shortest amount of time. Agents that aren't with the big syndicates can take longer to get homes sold costing the home owner money.

I use everything--the whole network kit and kaboodle--and pay extra to have featured listings so that my info is the only info on my listings. Why? So *I* get the calls and the *home owner* gets the exposure.

Yes, I get leads form Zillow and Trulia and Realtor by paying for the ad space. I know lots of brokers are mad about that and don't pay But I have learned that it pays off very well. This is an opportunity to have the best experience in the business..

Yes, I do hear from brokers, "What rights or protections can I receive or lose, and how can I control distribution of my listings or listing data?" I always go in and claim the listing and add more info so that mine is the one that will show up. I know if you claim your listing and post that you sold it you can have that on your profile. You can choose where you want to post on, and update your listings, add more info and branded video tours of the home.

Worry about lack of updating? It is true that some of us slack off and "forget" to update. You only have to enter the listing info once As you update it gets updated on all the syndication channels. In any case, you do know how to handle a client who may be annoyed if it happens a listing was not updated. On those portal channels they will link back to your company website.

When it comes to distribution, having your listing on many channels or portals increases the traffic to your site, gets your company brand and information in front of the consumer. Each syndicated portal has a variety of sites where they send listings. You can try the sites and it's easy to add or edit which destinations you choose.

Some ask if the site is reporting sales, do the rules/terms require the site to give the broker for the buyer and seller side credit? I know if you claim your listing and post that you sold it you can have that on your profile.

Syndicated sites are the popular places with the home buying and selling public, and usually the first place consumers go.

Paying to Win

Coldwell Banker, as others do, syndicates to third party sites so that their listings are seen by the most eyes. Not only that, Coldwell Banker, as others do, uses enhanced advertising of property on Trulia, Zillow, Realtor.com and Yahoo Real estate, to provide consumers, the maximum online exposure they could expect and surely deserve, and that essential competitive edge. Potential buyer leads and web traffic is not lost when your home is put in front of the largest audience. I myself, like Coldwell Banker, and feel confident that our tools help us to do best what we are hired to do -- sell your home, buy a home.

You get what you pay for.

Do the site's rules/terms guarantee there will not be competitive ads next to my listings you might ask? My answer is, no, that ad space is free game you have to buy it up if you want it you can pay them to have the contact be you but there is also google banner ads there which you can buy through google. Our job is to get the client the most money so we put it everywhere we allow z/t to do that we pay more to be featured listings so our clients home stands out even more.

Some Glossary and Encyclopedia Type Stuff from Z-A

• Zillow has had reports of 260,000 followers on Twitter, 1.3 million likes on Facebook, 49,000 followers on Instagram, 25,000 followers on Google Plus, and its website gets over 45 million unique visitors per month.

• Realtor.com has had reports of about 111,000 followers on Twitter, 96,000 likes on Facebook, 664 followers on Instagram, 10,000 followers on Google Plus, and its website generates about just over 22 million unique visitors per month.

• Zillow creates content with its blog for informative and educational tips but also fun and engaging.

• Realtor.com National Association for Realtors 23 million consumers is reported to have/mo, database of 4 million homes for sale or rent, 80% updated every 15 min, the rest updated 1-24 hrs

• TruliaZillow combined will probably the most highly trafficked real estate portal on the web a power house.

- Zillow had reports of 83 million users in 6/2014

- Trulia had reports of 54 million users in 6/2014

- Zillow acquired competitor Trulia.

- Zillow and Trulia combined was reported as made up of 89% traffic to top 15 websites in real estate category in 7/2014 and have been growing traffic.

- Zillow reported their listing agreement with ListHub will end 4/7 , but Zillow launched a new Data Dashboard which they believe will fill in and increase any loss of ListHub listings. The Data Dashboard, a list management and reporting platform, allows brokers to opt in or out of sending their listings to Zillow in one click, keep customized MLSD fields, automatically update their listings every 15 minutes, set lead routing rules include links to individual listing pages on their website, get free daily reports of listing performance metrics like search results, impressions, total listing views, total leads delivered. Brokers can access the Dashboard thru a URL sent by their MLS . The MLS must choose to implement the Dashboard for brokers to access it. The new Data Dashboard makes it easier to update and get up to date data directly rather than deal with 3rd parties like List Hub.

• ThreeWide Corp operates ListHub which is owned by Move,Inc which operates Realtor.com for the National Association of Realtors.

• Move was acquired by News Corp Rupert Murdock media empire . Move owns Three Wide which operates ListHub and Realtor.com which operates News Corp.

• Move is a subsidiary of News Corp which operates 30 million readers month including Realtor.com, Moving.com, Senior Housing Network.com, Door Steps Hub--access to what is reported as a comprehensive selection of homes for sale property records, mortgage resources, moving resources and more. Reports are that consumers spend more than 70 million minutes month on Move sites.

• Zillow has already begun experimenting with 3-D virtual tour technology which they expect is going to transform the real estate industry.

• ListTrac technology is often described as the google analytics for listings because it offers MLS brokers and agents their own dashboards with metrics that monitor performance of their listings. This feature allows members to share detailed data easily with customers and clients with a unique apples to apples comparison from each website that displays the participating brokers listing content. Listing agents can offer sellers both detailed market activity in a listing's local area as well as the online activity of their listing.

Final Thoughts

Just when you think there are far too many choices and changes, there is always more to come.

One project proposed for 2016 is known as the National Broker Portal Project, is a first national MLS consumer-facing listing portal. As of now, there is reported support from the Realty Alliance, franchise organizations, LeadingRE, CMLS members and COVE. The project is described as a means to use property links from consumer emails to their agents in local MLSs. They believe monthly traffic to begin at 20 million hits. Of course, like all plans, this one has its flaws, and no doubt will go through its permutations--which may or may not affect everything else!

Syndicated listings puts control of listings and where their listing appears, in the hands of brokers and agents and as with Zillow, these companies have continued to develop a friendlier role with brokers looking at them as perhaps partners and the source of information.

To be sure, there will be improvements-- new permutations, transparency, easier access and control of data, accuracy and updating. That's everything you need -- providing accurate and timely listings on these "extortion networks" to the millions of consumers who go to find or sell a home and connect with you.

Notes

Chapter 13

Facebook Lead Generation

Facebook- -it wired the world, it's the "bomb" as kids say, everywhere. Even my friend's 99 year old grandparent checks out Facebook with the grandkids. That's all the more reason why our social business in real estate should love using Facebook. For ads-- I am finding Facebook relatively cheap and terrific, a connecting heaven, and it's a pleasure too, in its all-pervasive way.

How Easy Can It Be?

I have a facebook page, https://www.facebook.com/Realestateagentboulde r, which is what I use to do my ads, so the adds come right from that page. Facebook is a simple and easy way for you to put your special touch out there with ads. They have many options which do a lot of work for you -- including getting great review posts to call attention to your page.

You have some choices with regard to where your ad is placed on Facebook:
- Desktop News Feed Advertisement
- Mobile News Feed Advertisement
- Right-Hand Column Advertisements
- Partner Mobile Apps

You might try different areas to see which performs best for you.

The Landing Page

You can use Listing to Leads, if you wish, to create your landing pages--this is a service that creates landing pages for you, or you can also use a

WordPress plugin in to create landing pages if you don't want to use the Listings to Leads service. Authority pro 3 is a WordPress plugin that creates simple landing pages or whatever else you choose to make the start simple and easy, and that also works for Facebook ads.

How Many Ads Do You Need and How Long?

I like having 5 different ads.5 seems to be the magic number to generate leads and let people get to know you along the way as they see each of the 5. It's a really successful way to grow client relationships and generate all those leads you want and need.

I have my ads run at the same time and kind of rotate-- so you can tell a story with your ads. See, a story, is fun, telling YOUR story, makes real estate more personal, right! And that's what you want for best connections and leads.

When I run the ads I will run them for 1 week at a time, 3-5 different ad groups. For each ad group I use a $5.00 figure per day. So for just $15 -25 dollars a day, this will usually keep me tied up with 3 or 4 leads a day, that I work through in my follow up process . It gets me super busy!

An Enticing Ad Plan

I create ads that entice with a "find out how much your home is worth" On my site it's this page: http://www.searchallproperties.com/propertyvaluation/ryan@myboulderhome.com/Boulder%2C+Colorado-106619?custom=2 What is My Home Worth?

That great page reads: "Find out why 30-40% of homes still go unsold even in this sellers market!" with a video to click on.

Additionally, the viewers click to "find out your home's current market value" which speedily takes them to the page that reads: "What is My Home Worth? Receive a custom evaluation for your home, including comparisons to other homes that have recently sold or are on the market. This guarantees you receive the most accurate information available. To find out what your home is worth, fill out the information below."

Beautiful! And to boost it all, my Facebook page includes the great addition about Coldwell Banker.."WHO IS THE MOST POWERFUL BRAND IN COLORADO REAL ESTATE?"

Then I create "open house" ads that go to the listing page, "just listed" ads, "sold" and "pending" ads can go here as well.

Client Raves and Testimonial Tributes

The testimonials and awesome client reviews from Zillow can go to a link on your listings page, putting you face to face with people you don't even know yet. This kind of word of mouth advertising does wonders to boost your credibility and likability.

Facebook can get you a tab from Zillow to do this. You do need a Zillow account and with that account sign in, go to "my agent hub" top right, "select profile", under your name click "request a review". You can send this to clients or, see "send multiple requests at once" on the bottom, and that's how to collect them all.

To get that Tab on your Facebook business page, go to "agent Hub", click on "widget Facebook app", Then click on Real Estate apps for Facebook page". Next you have to click "Review Tab". You can email a person, or click on "Listing Tab" and get reviews for all the contacts. Great stuff, for free!

While I'm talking about tabs for Facebook, if you have your real estate facebook page you're all set, otherwise, you will first need to go to your personal profile. Along the top of the profile page you will see a blue bar. At the very right of this bar is a small icon that looks like a downward-facing triangle. Click on this icon and then click on "Create page." Click on "local business or place," choose real estate for your category, fill in the other information, and then click "get started." Once you have your page set up, you will automatically have a review section. It can be found under the "More" button right below your cover photo. Just click "reviews" and your clients click the "write a review" button to add their review.

So I am going to walk you through the very simple steps to making those 5 different ads work for you!

As I said, but it bears repeating, they all run at the same time and kind of rotate so you can tell a story with your ads.

"The Walk"-- How To Advertise on Facebook Creating those Ads

Now, on your facebook site you will see on the bottom a link to **"create an Ad"** so click.
That takes you to a page with support, if you need it, but I'm here with your support. This is simple so let's now go to the green box in the upper right-**"Create an Ad"**, and now, we're cookin'.

This takes you to **Step 1. Create Your Campaign.**
The first thing you do for your campaign is choose what you want people to do when they see your ad.
So go to **"ad creation"** and now choose an **"advertising objective."**

Type in or select from the dropdown what you want to advertise. The choices are:
Send people to your website
Increase conversions on your website Use this objective If you're seeking to generate leads through a lead capture form. This is also used in conjunction with a Facebook pixel to track how many users convert on your site.
Boost your posts

Promote your Page
Get installs of your app
Increase engagement in your app
Reach people near your business
Raise attendance at your event: If you have a special open house or event, use this option to share the event with a larger audience.
Get people to claim your offer
Get video views
Use the Page post engagement objective to boost your post.

Then you'll type in the URL that you want people to go to.
OK ready for Continue click.

You can track how your ads are working to meet your advertising objective in Ads Manager.

So now let's click on **"Send people to your website"** and we're already to **Step 2.**
Step 2 is **"Create Your Ad Account"** so enter your account info--Country, Currency and Time Zone.
All your ads, billing and reporting data will be recorded in this currency and time zone. If you find you need to change these, you'll need to create a new ad account.

If you have multiple ad accounts, you can select which one you want to create an ad for when you choose an advertising objective.

OK we're going full speed ahead to:
 Step 3: "Create Your Ad Set", "Who do you want your ads to reach?"

When you create an ad set, you'll define the audience that will see the ads in your ad set. Choosing a relevant audience for your business is important because your ad will only be shown to people who match the criteria you select.

Facebook offers a selection of audience targeting options for a custom audience if you want. You can choose from one or a combination of them depending on your needs, or in order to reach people who have a specific kind of connection to your Page, app or event, so that's "connections".

Or, just go ahead to:

"Location" add country, state, city or zip,
 "Age" 22+ or what is appropriate,
"Gender"
"Languages" and there are **"More Demographics"** if you wish.

To the right a box shows your **Audience Definition** measure or your potential reach number. Most recommend under 50,000 and that 17,000 is fine. This helps you monitor the effectiveness of your target audience. It lets you know when your search may be too specific (red), too broad (yellow), or somewhere in a good range (green).

Next, **"Interest"** and **"Behaviors"** areas allows you to plug in more customization.

Now to a bit of spending.

"How Much do you want to spend?" comes next.
Your ad set budget is the maximum amount you want to spend.
If you choose a daily budget, the amount you enter is the maximum you'll spend each day. If you choose a lifetime budget, the amount you enter is the maximum you'll spend during the lifetime of your ad set.
Your ad set will either run continuously starting today or within a date range you select.

So now schedule say $5.00 a day for a week and plug in your dates.

The cost of your advertising on Facebook depends on the size of your audience and your budget.
Facebook ad costs are all up to you

Now, to the right you will see **"Estimated Daily Reach"** This is the total number of people in your selected audience who are active on Facebook each day.

Okay, now we can get creative with **step 4:**
STEP 4: CREATE YOUR AD
Select the images you want to use
You can create multiple ads.
Each image you add will create a different ad in your ad set. After your campaign starts, you can monitor how audiences respond to the different images.
The recommended image size is 1200 x 628 pixels

Add up to 6 images. You can upload new images, use images from your library, or search for free professional images from Shutterstock.

So browse, search, upload and reposition away.

Okay, now we come to **"What text and links do you want to use?"**
You can create a Facebook Page to represent your business in News Feed. Your ad will link to your site, and show as coming from your Facebook Page. Or, Turn Off News Feed Ads.

Next is that all important **"Headline,"** that catchy come on. So add a headline that grabs people's attention and tells them what your ad is about.

"Text" is an opportunity to tell people a bit more about what you're promoting. Put just 2 things you want here-- a short sentence about your listing--just the best highlights of the listing. With a little blurb you get phone numbers and so many text leads

Next, choose a landing view — the place you want folks to land when they click your ad.

Now there is an optional **"call to Action"** button. Choose the action you want people to take when they see your ad.

And still there are **"Advanced Options"**

At the News Feed Link Description you can describe why people should visit your website.

To the right you'll see a "**Create a Facebook Page**
to show your ads in News Feed
or Turn Off News Feed Ads"

We're at the end! So before you send it off, you can review it with the review button.

And then, "Place Order."

There is a reason why Mark Zuckerberg is one of the most successful entrepreneurs of our age. Facebook is the master at connecting, at bringing all of the parts together to create excitement, engagement and community. And all it takes to start building that is 5 little ads, and 25.00 a day!

Notes

Chapter 14

Goody Goody Google

The Overview

For just a quickie overview of the processes with ads and Google, here's what I do: We create ads in Google that go to the lead capture website (I use the Marketleader website). On the Marketleader site you are able to direct the ad to the page it will be sent to. Marketleader is a CRM and lead generating website such as in mybouldercohome.com

My ads will become the search ads, and are the text ads with the extensions that you'll see and specify when you put in your ad.

But here is what I do a little differently, and will get you many more leads than the ads alone – it is my special "one-two punch."

You will also use a separate campaign that is the display network which is where we create banner ads that show up on different websites, which then sends people back to our lead capture website. You might start looking at sample banner ads are here http://www.chooseabanner.com/gallery

The ads are created or uploaded to Google AdWords, then link back to the Marketleader website.

I use fiverr.com to make the display ads that I upload to Google Adwords where it can be plugged in at the display ads banner ads place.

They display ads combined with Google AdWords will create a "banner day" for your business!

Ad for Search Campaign

Okay. Now, this is how a regular ad group is done for a search campaign.

It's real easy. You just start right off on Google AdWords, and go to "settings."

Now you get your campaign name setting. There you can choose what devices you will want that search on. I like to check Search Google Only and I check "Search Network Only," "Computers" and Tablets with Browsers."

Now you click on "Keywords" and you check off many. But watch out for the too broad search, the broad search is the default, so be more exacting and use exact matches.

Next you have your "Ad Extensions" which give you your sitelinks, and location extensions.

Now you go to the top and search for what you want-- for me it's "find a home in Boulder".

This is the add that I type into Google in the search ads section

Search only

Boulder homes 500k-700k

Find all available homes for sale in Boulder

View Photos, Details, Maps & More!

And then you want to send people to that page, so then plug in your URL that will send people to your page.

Next you want to get to your "Ad Extensions" and under that are Location extensions, and sitelink extensions, call extensions, app, review and callout extensions--add what you want.

Okay, now Edit your Ad Group sitelink extension. You go to New Sitelink. You want to Link your text, and put in your destination URL

And now, you're done

The Display Ad

Now I'm going to do a quick walk through of the Display for you, different from the search.

First select "All Features." It's a display so it will show on all of the websites real estate related, Zillow Trulia, whatever you want.

Now you'll see "Targeted Locations." You pick what you need +25 miles around it.

OK now to "Edit Locations." Here you get a cool kind of map that lets you see clearly where your ad will show up inside this area and anyone looking in this area.

Now get back to "Settings" and back to "Location Options."

I choose English since that's all of the languages I speak.

For "Bid Strategy" I like to focus on clicks. That is about how many clicks you want on your ad daily. And that will determine your budget. So if you want 100 clicks and each click costs about 5cents, you need to budget $5 a day. You just multiply the cost per click or CPC by the number of clicks you want. So then for your Budget you plug in $5.00 a day, $50 a day, whatever you want to do.

Now comes "Delivery Method." Here I want to make sure I just send to desk top devices. Or if you want to do mobile.

Okay, now go to your "display Network Tab" and then to "Targeting and Display Keywords."

Here you want to get 500 words. I type in Boulder real estate and scroll down to the bottom and copy those words, keep clicking on links down there until you get to 500. I create a list of 500 words or so about real estate and my town Boulder homes for sale, Boulder CO , etc.

Then you put that in your key word box which will trigger where the adds get shown so when zillow and trulia have ads for your area the adword display ads show up there as well as lots of other local spaces.

Then, go back to your "Campaign page" and then "Upload."

Or, you can do placements where you want your ad to appear... on Realtor.com, Zillow Trulia, etc. You may need to pay more for them and need separate campaign pages.

Okay, now in "Settings," this will get at inside the area you want.

Now go to the Ad Tab. Here's where you upload. So I go to fiverr.com to get my ads made. You can click to see sample ads--hundreds on realtor.com--and send what you like to fiverr and say here, look at this, make me one like this.

Then you're in, you upload your ad and you're in business.

Here's how to advertise from AdWords

Go to AdWords
Click into the Ads tab and select "new ad"
Then "display ad builder" from the drop down.

Now select a template and there are 100s there for you to choose.

Next name your ad and that name is not for anyone else to see just for you to identify it.

Okay now enter your ad text. This is choosing your font and colors.

Include a call to action in the text.

Now for headline, you'll plug in your descriptions-- your font, headline text, color, and description.

Now select an image from your own files.

Next comes a fill out box for display, and destination URL for your landing page.

And also a select ad sizes. Here it automatically creates your ad in multiple sizes.

Now it's ready!

AdWords Add Rank and how it Adds up

Naturally you've been on Google searches, like everyone, and saw the sponsored links in a yellow area on top of the rest of the results. This is what happens with Google AdWords and there, on top is what you want as your best bet for traffic to your website and leads. But how to get there?

Google AdWords are not just there on top automatically. The gist and the trick behind them is about the words you need and want for your ads. AdWords are Google's text based ads that are on top when people search for those magic keywords.

The AdWords system is said to visit and evaluate landing information regularly. Your adwords quality is said to help with your AdRank.

So the AdWords secret is that in order for your ad to show up where you want it you bid against other ads for your search words and you only pay if someone clicks and then visits your site.

Landing Page Affects

Your landing page is quite important, and also affects your Quality Score, Ad Rank and advertising costs. So you want to make sure your info on your landing page is useful with unique features to your site and easy to find your contact info

Google talks about 3 main parts that tell about your landing page Quality Score: relevant and original content, meaning that users find what you promise easily and relevant to your ad text and keywords with useful info and unique info. And all of course, optimized for search engine users.
Strong engaging, compelling up to date headlines.
So make sure your info on your landing page is useful with unique features to your site
and easy to find your contact info.

Also, a powerful Landing Page will:
- Focus on benefits not features to answer a viewers question: what's in it for me?
- Show how their life will be better or easier.
- Have transparency and trustworthiness, and ease of navigation .

Some users have recommended telling an interesting fun personal story or mention something in a relevant and dramatic way for interest to avoid dullness.

Quality Here is a Score to Keep--Quality Score

Your quality score is something Google assigns to you based on your landing pages, and it can lower your ad costs and give you a better page position if your landing page is great. Every time someone searches Google, an AdWords auction is happening. And every ad with a keyword match to that search query competes in the auction. And then, how well you as an advertiser competes is based on your Ad Rank which is Ad Rank =Quality Score and Bid.

Including Ad Rank in the Formulations of Quality for Top Placement

There have been suggestions with math computations that some find useful in AdRanking, believing that the highest Ad Rank gets top spot and so on.
You as an advertiser pay the lowest amount necessary to best the Ad Rank of the competitor below you. And the formula for the money is
$$\$\$=AdRank \text{ to best/Quality Score}+ \$0.01$$
So by example, you want to be in 1st position. You over bid the keyword to say $100/click. Ad Rank =800=(QS 8*$100 Bid)
To beat you a competitor needs to get an ad rank above 800, so even if they had a QS10 keyword they would have to bid $80.01/click to get top listing.

But, lets say the competitor bid $10/click. So then the amount you pay in auction would be: Ad Rank to beat=100=(QS10*$10 Bid) which is
$12.51=100/8 + $0.01 =(100 Ad Rank to best/our QS8 + $0.01
So even though you bid $100, you pay just $12.51

Signing Up for Google AdWords Account.

Remember this is free and you only pay when you start running ads.
Your keyword research counts here and you want the best triggers from those words.
Google suggest starting broad and narrowing down later. Don't use words that a customer wouldn't use but do think of the words that they will use.
Log into your AdWord Account
Go to Tools and Analysis and click on keyword tool
Type in your keyword and ad words will come back for you with a number of searches connected for it.
You click on keyword suggestions at the top and you can also get other keywords to consider.
Next lick on the campaign link at the menu top and choose create a new campaign which takes you to your campaign set up page.
On your campaign set up page you plug in your campaign name.
And your campaign type. Know that the default on Google's paid search run on both Google Search and Google Display. But it is recommended to start off changing to "search network only" which is more targeted.
For Locations use the targeting and click on let me choose and then on advanced search.

Budget is next. This is the amount you pay per click and your maximum daily budget. Google says the average conversion rate is 5%. So to figure it you think about what you can pay for a new client, say $50.00 With about a 5% chance of getting a new client about 20 people have to click. So then you divide $50 by 20 and your starting level budget is $2.50 a click as your default bid.

Ad extras. This is for your address, phone, other links. These do not cost you extra.

Now write your ad.

The headline should grab attention and what you are offering

Description in line 1 should spark their interest

Description in line 2 should get them wanting your service

Then the Display URL should get them to decide and act.

You can come up with 3 or so ads by clicking ads and then choose "new ad". Google automatically rotates your ads so you can see which one does best for you.

Let your campaign run a week for good data to judge which ads and keywords are working for you.

Google Analytics

You can link a Google Analytic to your AdWords Account to see your customer activity.

First check that your Google Account has Edit Permission and Administrative Access for the AdWords Account for the Google Linking Places to link your AdWords to Google Analytics.

After you made the link you can remove the permissions.

Sign in to your AdWords Account
Click Tools tab and Google Analytics
Click the Admin tab at the top
In the Account column select Analytics Account that has the property you want to work with your AdWords Account
Then go to the "Property" column and choose the Analytics property you want to and click the AdWords Linking
Select the check box next to any AdWords accounts you want to link with your Analytics property
Click "Continue"
Next in the Link Configuration enter title for your group of linked AdWords accounts.
Now select the Analytics Views where you want the data available.
Now click Link Accounts.
Done.

How to track your conversions

You can install Google's free Conversion Tracking
You just copy and past a tracking snippet into your website's source code.
The report you get lets you know the steps your visitors take before getting a conversion.
To get these reports you go to the Tool and Analysis Tab in AdWords, and choose Conversions.
Click on Search Funnels on the left.
So this way you can get rid of keywords that aren't performing and keep the ones that are.

A Note about Key Word Relevancy

There are lots of different opinions and advice about all of this. Some find it is important to be concerned about key word relevancy to your ads. And to use perfect message matches of your ad with your key word or words, which should be a person's search word or words. A formula talked about is Higher relevancy = higher click-through rate = higher Quality Score = lower cost per click = lower cost per conversion. To help ensure this there are recommendations for having 2 different ads in an ad group that you can test to see which one works better for you. So to make this happen, the recommendations are: Headline: Include keyword in headline.

Description line 1: Talk about benefits and features. Description line 2: Talk about benefits. Call to action!
Display URL: YourDomain.com/Keyword

People searching are going through search engines that are determining a "quality score" for where it will be placed, and the score, includes your ad copy ranking, which is partly a ranking based on your copy and your targeted keyword. The belief is that if your ad reads, for example, Buy a home in Boulder, but you target the phrase homes in Boulder, your quality score can be low. So the suggestion is to make sure your keywords can trigger your ads is to rephrase the targeted keyword phrase in your ad along with details about its benefit.

To make sure your keywords are triggering the right ads to show, suggestions are to do keyword diagnoses. So to do this, go to your AdWords account, click on the "Details" button and then "Keyword diagnosis."

A Tip from an Eye Tracking Study

Just a note to mention that a special eye tracking study was made regarding display URL's in PPC (pay-per-click) ads. The study clearly showed that the display URL in PPC ads captures a significant gaze time on an ad. The study also showed that display URLs have a real impact on numbers of click-thrus.

Because of Google's powerful tools and user friendly interfaces, you can get up and running with a display ad campaign easily, without tons of time and costs.

With this handy tool and a little practice, in only a few minutes you will be creating high-quality image ads to support your AdWords campaigns, and making the most of what Google has to offer.

Notes

Chapter 15

Freakishly "Freeish" Leads with Links and SEO

SEO--a boon to all businesses these past few years--statistics shows that a good SEO strategy is the most effective source for anyone who wants new customers.

The data shows that organic search is THE place people look--the largest draw for both revenue and traffic for any industry including real estate. And this is expected to continue and grow this coming year.

But what the search engines are really looking for changes constantly, and SEO has become as much an art as a science.

Here are some of my best tips for thinking about your SEO and the links to make them work for you. As you will see, one of your greatest challenges, will be to keep up with Google changes that happen as fast as anything else changes in our lives.

But here we go with some of the latest thinking.

1. SEO has become a discipline complete with traditional marketing plans for everyone.

2. Its important to merge your quantitative data with your search topics and couple that with

who your target audience is and what exactly is useful for them....along with seeing what your competition is doing on demand topics and what you can do better than them.

3. You need to focus on finding new keywords to target your audience, and bring them to your content. Get into their heads, if you were them, what would you be looking for?. And as for your content, there is a lot of talk and belief about blogs and web content as key to maximize your value and visibility. Content needs to always be fresh, meaty, substantial, honest and transparent.

4. Most important to Google is user experience and quality. In terms of experience-- time and speed is of the essence so no slow loadings, quick ease in navigating. Google is said to want sites to do content in under 1 second. Quality is really the main objective now for Google. Google uses Google Knowledge to think about your facts. This often results in Google's Display Boxes on the right. But aside from that, Google wants to give everyone the most specific answer to their question or search. Google will favor and reward you as a teacher, a good communicator with your reader or searcher, not just because you sound smart.

4. You need to get into new markets. Mobile SEO is always recommended because it has already been the years of mobile, more than desk top

media in time spent. What people see when they look is important to see it well in small and large sizes. Multimedia is the life--text, videos, blogs, etc.

New Ideas about Keywords

1. Definitely placement of keywords--in the header, your meta information is highest priority rather than frequency. Also some description of your company to back those keywords up in those high priority places.

2. Google wants the meaning of those words, they interpret your website data to see what you really are offering and especially, to see that you are an authority in your niche. Authority is a big word nowadays for Google. Backing up authority are recommendations to title appropriately, use a header bar, a crawlable site map, and to interlock your inner content pages.

Now Why Should You Care about SEO anyway?

One way or another, you can't avoid it, SEO and links produce and earn listings. And you want them. Google and the Internet of course is run by HTML. Links are important to SEO search engine organization. Google and other search engines gives credit, extra credit to websites with good quality back links, relevant websites and in their results pages, you hope your searchers will see you on top. Links and success in search engine results pages depends not only on your own site but getting links from other sites to your site, effectively.

Couple of Tools to Mention for Linking

There is a Back link Builder Tool that is designed to help you search for websites with related themes to your website. But I actually helped you already with that job with a large suggested list of links below.

There is a Domain Status Tool that displays the back links of a domain on Google, Yahoo and MSN which helps keep track of back links and which sites are linking back to you.

What Goes into Google Ranking?

The exact formula for gaining the best Google ranking is as mysterious as the location of the Lost Ark.

Many experts claim to know, but no one is really so sure. But here are the elements that certainly go into it. As Google grows and changes, emphasis on one or the other may strengthen or weaken, but all still seem to play a part in it.

1. Anchor text. When a link uses a keyword in the text of a hyperlink its called a quality anchor text. You want a link with your actual desired keyword or keyword phrase , but don't overdo it, or you may be sandboxed for anchor text abuse. Just the right use of anchor text is believed to boost your quality links score. Which, is said to better your ranking. There is a MozRank that shows how popular a web page is and which has better rankings.

2. Local popularity. Links from your topic specific community matters.

3. Social sharing--Facebook, Google+ Twitter, word press blogs. This is controversial but is said to figure into the search engine algorithms too.

4. Link Bit is often considered high quality, trustworthy and authority proving that is supposed to boost rankings. This is something wild and fun that goes viral but has useful information.

5. You need good site structure, and plenty of text links pointing to each program on your site. Rich information on your site with cool in depth articles are said to get the chance of high ranking.

6. Links on mainstream news sites, related industry sites, authority sites, university and government resources, brands that are trusted have a lot of links for you. See my suggested list below

7. No nos and penalty material are: syndicated material (sometimes), directory links, forums, widgets, paid links.

8. Understand that, your SEO and linking won't be mastered in a day, but, like that quest for the Lost Ark, it's an ever growing process of small steps! Pick a few of the links below and place articles or posts with a link to your website.

Suggested Places to Get Freeish Links

1.   realestateads.nytimes.com/
2.   olx.in/real-estate-cat-16
3.   loot.com/property
4.   online.wsj.com/ad/advertiseproperty.html
5.   freepropertyads.co.za/
6.   propertyads.co.uk/
7.   propertyadsja.com/
8.   kspropertyads.com/
9.   century21jm.com/
10.   adverts.ie/property/282/
11.   domain.com.au/Public/List.aspx

12.   realestatebook.com/agents/usa/va/harrisonburg/linda-whitmore-id15526
13.   isgproperty.sg/
14.   h88.com.sg/
15.   property.singaporeexpats.com/place-property-ad
16.   ezproperty.sg/free-posting
17.   stproperty.sg/
18.   propertyhub.com.sg/faq/cat/posting-guides/45.html
19.   singapore.locanto.sg/post/W/
20.   realtormag.realtor.org/sales-and-marketing/feature/article/2013/01/getting-your-sellers-pay-for-advertising
21.   prumt.com/resources/seller_services/
22.   realestateabc.com/homeselling/
23.   jenman.com.au/BS_Advertising.php
24.   cbc.ca/news/canada/ottawa/fake-real-estate-ads-prey-on-buyer-desire-for-home-deal-1.2445689
25.   profit.ndtv.com/news/your-money/article-indias-real-estate-market-time-for-the-bubble-to-burst-371745
26.   classmart.post-gazette.com/
27.   youtube.com/watch?v=7OaGKdZXBiE
28.   buzzfeed.com/adamdavis/real-estate-ads-that-totally-nailed-it
29.   sellingguide.realestate.com.au/advertising/

30. nytimes.com/pages/realestate/
31. nypost.com/real-estate/
32. palmbeachpost.com/s/classifieds/
33. washingtonpost.com/classifieds
34. mediakit.denverpost.com/realEstate.html
35. boston.com/realestate/placead/faq/
36. postlets.com/
37. realtor.com/
38. homefinder.com/
39. moneycontrol.com/news/real-estate/property-pricesdownward-trend-best-time-to-invest_1023588.html
40. globalpropertyguide.com/Asia/India
41. business.mapsofindia.com/investment-industry/real-estate-investment.html
42. realtyplusmag.com/
43. st701.com/
44. articles.economictimes.indiatimes.com/2014-01-31/news/46870333_1_indian-origin-rupee-loans-nro-nre
45. businesstoday.intoday.in/story/how-to-invest-in-real-estate-for-steady-returns-in-long-run/1/187432.html
46. boston.com/realestate/placead/
47. sg-house.com/classifieds/free-property-classified-ads-buy-sell-and-rent-houses-and-rooms/
48. everstonecapital.com/

49.   businesstoday.intoday.in/story/buying-property-here-are-risks-that-you-must-avoid/1/187425.html

50.   realtormag.realtor.org/sales-and-marketing/feature/article/2012/04/write-ads-sell

51.   propertyox.com/free-singapore-property-listings-website-property-advertising/

52.   http://adsnity.com/top/real-estate/

53.   forbesindia.com/article/the-big-questions-for-2014/is-the-real-estate-bubble-big-enough-to-naturally-burst-in-2014/36797/1

54.   placeanad.latimes.com/residential-real-estate-for-sale-listing

55.   adrealestateinc.com/

56.   ebayclassifieds.com/

57.   loyalclassified.com/

58.   rentcompass.com/free-rental-ads

59.   pinterest.com/loyalclassified/post-free-classifieds-ads-search-free-classified-a/

60.   adlandpro.com/

61.   *www.therealestateclassified.com/*

62.   zillow.com/post-rental-listings/

63.   thatrentalsite.com/post

64.   rent-index.com/

65.   olx.in/

66.   longisland.com/classifieds/

67.   mrrental.ca/

68. homebuying.knoleggs.com/post-apartment-ads-online-for-free.htm
69. dir.yahoo.com/business_and_economy/classifieds/
70. nj.com/classifieds/free/
71. kijiji.ca/h-halifax/80010
72. nhvtclassified.com/
73. craigslist.com/
74. quikr.com/
75. ksl.com/?nid=47
76. adpost.com/
77. Adsnity.com
78. claz.org/top-classifieds-sites.html
79. olx.co.tz/
80. classifieds.mlive.com/
81. rentdigs.com/Common/OwnerInfo.aspx
82. studentrent.com/rental-advertising/
83. classifieds.bangkokpost.com/
84. padlister.com/
85. *www.4realestateclassifieds.com/*
86. sublet.com/post.asp
87. khojle.in/
88. onlinechandha.com/
89. onbip.com/
90. http://adsnity.com/top/real-estate/
91. freeads.in/
92. discoverlebanon.com/en/deals/
93. londonon.craigslist.ca/

94. boston.craigslist.org/

95. apps.postindependent.com/utils/c2/app/v2/index.php?do=category&internetCode=11

96. maine.olx.com/

97. hallolondon.co.uk/

98. classifieds.triblive.com/

99. classifieds.nola.com/

100. facebook.com/freeads.nxt/info

101. rentalads.com/add_rental/

102. adsector.us/

103. fredericknewspost.com/wrapper/classifieds/

104. commonfloor.com/list-your-property

105. oodle.military.com/

106. thetoptens.com/best-free-classifieds-websites/

107. mcgill.ca/classified/

108. wantedwants.com/

109. bangalorerealestate.indiagrid.com/

110. 5ndme.com/

111. glisters.com/postfreeads.html

112. junkmail.co.za/cape-town

113. azcentral.com/class/

114. classifieds.orange.mu/

115. starclassifieds.com/

116. classifieds.vancouversun.com/

117. vancouver.nortad.com/

118. gumtree.com/london

119. expatads.com/20-Indonesia/posts/5-Housing/330-Furnished-Apartments
120. betogel.com/search/free-america-ads-find-and-post-all-kind-of-classifieds
121. metrowny.com/free_classifieds_search.php
122. bozemandailychronicle.com/classifieds/
123. classifieds.foreignercn.com/
124. lancasteronline.com/classifieds/
125. commonfloor.com/list-your-property
126. pinedaleonline.com/classifieds.htm
127. classifieds.silive.com/
128. miamiherald.com/classified-ads/
129. chicagoil.global-free-classified-ads.com/
130. classifieds.pembinavalleyonline.com/
131. craigslist.com.sg/
132. hongkong.mycads.com/
133. argentina.gumpul.com/
134. classifieds.foreignercn.com/
135. slideshare.net/99dealr/free-online-ad-posting-site-in-india-online-business-promotion-in-india-made-easy
136. rentseeker.ca/rental-marketing.aspx
137. apps.aspentimes.com/utils/c2/app/v2/index.php?do=category&internetCode=11
138. gurgaon.briskom.com/
139. belize.gumpul.com/
140. bnd.com/classified-ads/
141. classmart.post-gazette.com/

142. helptobuynsell.com/
143. freeadsindia.in/
144. http://adsolist.com/free-advertising-sites-bangalore-kolkata-india-classifieds-post-free-ads/

One of the Latest Reports

A recent report about getting online leads from various channels showed that agents did find a percentage of results from them, and other agents feel it is a benefit to spend more time trying to tap into unpaid online leads through marketing channels. To make the most of these leads many suggested what helps is:

•   To beef up your agent profiles and to interact on Facebook.

•   Respond to an online lead quickly, like within 5 minutes, track them to determine your ROI, nurture them until closing. Poor follow up, prejudging validity of leads and lack of urgency were causes of poorer conversion.

•   Have a good CRM that incubates the leads that are not quite ready to engage, because some come through but can take 6-12 months of incubation.

You know where you want to be, so use links, keep on top of your game, and you'll get there.

Congratulations,

You now know more information about online marketing, SEO and PPC than most of your peers and certainly your competitors.

Armed with this knowledge you now must take action and implement. This may seem like a daunting task, but implementing portions of your newfound knowledge can make huge changes in your revenues and how your business looks and feels. Often times the biggest factor holding you back from success is knowing when to ask for what you want!

So what do you want?

If you want your business to be the same in the years to come as it is now, then continue doing exactly what you are doing now. However, knowing that your competitors are going to take advantage of the leverage the Internet provides to grow their business – I daresay, if you do not take action, your business will not look the same but will be smaller, with a shrinking base of customers and revenues.

The landscape for local search is still the Wild West,. Right now in your sector or market, there is a land grab happening. If you need help, if you want your business to look different in the future, have more customers, make more revenue and ultimately you have more fun, then ask for it.

Now is the time for your future success and all the prosperity you desire!

Sincerely,

Ryan & Sondra Harper

Notes

Notes

76444359R00086

Made in the USA
Columbia, SC
04 September 2017